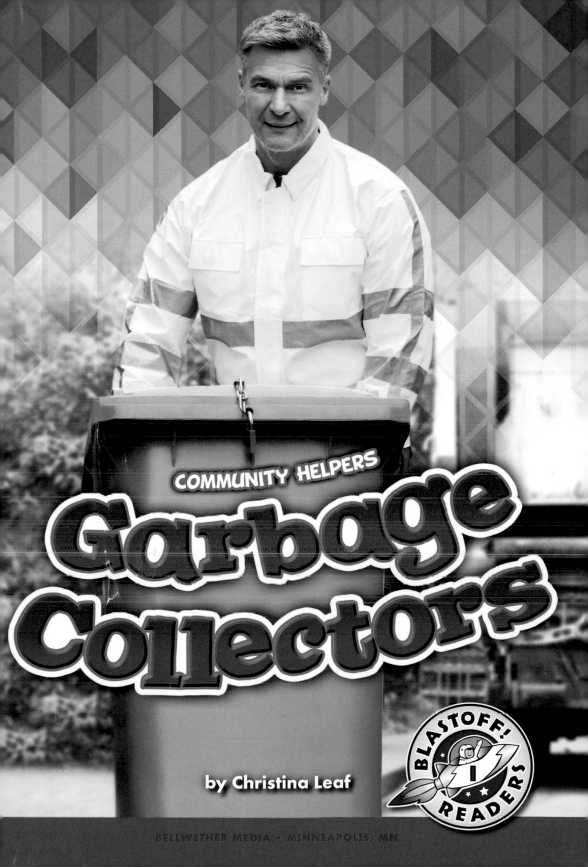

COMMUNITY HELPERS

Garbage Collectors

by Christina Leaf

BELLWETHER MEDIA • MINNEAPOLIS, MN

Note to Librarians, Teachers, and Parents:

Blastoff! Readers are carefully developed by literacy experts and combine standards-based content with developmentally appropriate text.

Level 1 provides the most support through repetition of high-frequency words, light text, predictable sentence patterns, and strong visual support.

Level 2 offers early readers a bit more challenge through varied simple sentences, increased text load, and less repetition of high-frequency words.

Level 3 advances early-fluent readers toward fluency through increased text and concept load, less reliance on visuals, longer sentences, and more literary language.

Level 4 builds reading stamina by providing more text per page, increased use of punctuation, greater variation in sentence patterns, and increasingly challenging vocabulary.

Level 5 encourages children to move from "learning to read" to "reading to learn" by providing even more text, varied writing styles, and less familiar topics.

Whichever book is right for your reader, Blastoff! Readers are the perfect books to build confidence and encourage a love of reading that will last a lifetime!

This edition first published in 2019 by Bellwether Media, Inc.

No part of this publication may be reproduced in whole or in part without written permission of the publisher. For information regarding permission, write to Bellwether Media, Inc., Attention: Permissions Department, 6012 Blue Circle Drive, Minnetonka, MN 55343.

Library of Congress Cataloging-in-Publication Data

Names: Leaf, Christina, author.
Title: Garbage Collectors / by Christina Leaf.
Description: Minneapolis, MN : Bellwether Media, Inc., [2019] | Series: Blastoff! Readers. Community Helpers | Includes bibliographical references and index.
Identifiers: LCCN 2017057410 (print) | LCCN 2017059201 (ebook) | ISBN 9781626178984 (hardcover : alk. paper)| ISBN 9781681035352 (ebook)
Subjects: LCSH: Refuse collectors–Juvenile literature. | Refuse collection–Juvenile literature.
Classification: LCC HD8039.R46 (ebook) | LCC HD8039.R46 L43 2019 (print) | DDC 628.4/42023–dc23
LC record available at https://lccn.loc.gov/2017057410

Editor: Rebecca Sabelko   Designer: Brittany McIntosh

Printed in the United States of America, North Mankato, MN.

Table of Contents

The truck pulls up to the house. The **garbage** collector grabs the trash bags.

The bags fall
into the truck.
The collector
hops back on.
Next stop!

What Are Garbage Collectors?

Garbage collectors pick up waste and **recycling** in cities and towns.

They take the waste to dumps or **landfills**. Special centers take recycling.

landfill

What Do Garbage Collectors Do?

Garbage collectors follow **routes**. They empty **bins** at each stop.

bin

Many collectors
must lift the
bins themselves.
Some empty bins
with a special lift
on a truck.

Garbage Collector Gear

reflective vest   gloves   earplugs   truck

lift

15

Recycling and
waste go in
different bins.
Collectors make
sure they
do not mix.

⚠ CAUT

KERBSIDE CO

IN PROGR

VEHICLE CON

STOPPI

What Makes a Good Garbage Collector?

These workers are strong. Bins can be heavy.

Garbage Collector Skills

- ✓ good drivers
- ✓ not bothered by smells
- ✓ strong
- ✓ speedy

19

Garbage collectors
must be able to
handle bad smells.
Trash stinks!

CHALLENGE
immobilier

21

Glossary

bins

containers that hold waste

recycling

items that can be made into something new

garbage

items that have been thrown out

routes

paths that are commonly traveled

landfills

places where trash is dumped

To Learn More

AT THE LIBRARY

Alexander, Richard. *What Do Garbage Collectors Do?* New York, N.Y.: PowerKids Press, 2016.

Kenan, Tessa. *Hooray for Garbage Collectors!* Minneapolis, Minn.: Lerner Publications, 2018.

Murray, Julie. *Garbage Trucks.* Minneapolis, Minn.: Abdo Kids, 2016.

ON THE WEB

Learning more about garbage collectors is as easy as 1, 2, 3.

1. Go to www.factsurfer.com.

2. Enter "garbage collectors" into the search box.

3. Click the "Surf" button and you will see a list of related web sites.

With factsurfer.com, finding more information is just a click away.

Index